MY FATHER IS SATURN

Poetry to Return to

Bugg Davis

b.d

You taught me when to use the sling.

May the stone land between the eyes of our giants.

Contents

PART 03. THE RETURN
(GENESIS 2:1-3)

PREFACE

The story that I want to tell you starts in 2001, in North Mississippi, in a double wide trailer out in the country. This is where I was raised.

Early in life, my father was a construction worker and he spent most of his weekends in a duck blind or a bass boat. He used to say he didn't need to go to church because he could find God in nature just as good as he could in a pew.

It was my mother who took me and my sister to church. It was my mother, in her prayer room, in the rose colored world inside of her head, through her mostly gentle, but constant insistence, that led my father back to the hymn books and hallelujahs.

That, and a pipe smashed into the side of his head one day when he was at work. It left him couch-locked for weeks. That time on the couch was his time in the belly of the whale. And he emerged a new man, marked by God, with his Capricorn tendencies thrusting him towards the top of the Southern Baptist Kingdom.

My father is a leader. It's in his DNA. No matter where his life ended up, there was never another choice in his mind. So after he returned to the church, my family quickly became a "ministry family".

This is the point where my sister, Shelby, and I had to learn to share our parents. At the time, I rarely thought of it that way, but hindsight is 20/20, and anyone who has been in a "ministry family" knows the sacrifices that come with that.

I was 8 when I committed my life to Jesus Christ, snot-nosed at the kitchen table, telling my parents I was afraid the devil was going to kill me. My parents assured me that when I became a child of God, nothing could harm me until he was ready for me to "come home". That was enough for me at the time. My sister's journey down the aisle and into the baptistry came soon after, and my father's kingdom expanded.

The youth group grew 3x its size and we created a youth band, which stirred up a number of verbal altercations in church meetings, where I watched my father wage war against gatekeepers and usher in new traditions.

He showed up and shielded every kid's innocence and we showed up with him. Every Sunday, every Wednesday, every day of the week if we had to.

This went on for years. My parents created, developed, and established summer youth camps for churches statewide. They drove car loads of teenagers from one end of Mississippi to the other, and they opened our home to kids in transitory situations. My parents never turned anyone away. They gave and gave and gave and they asked us to give with them.

I sunk my teeth into all of it; I loved all the things my father loved, in longing for his attention. I hand fed my sense of value through acts of service —and sacrifice—but it was more than just ego.

I believed. I knew God was real before I knew the church existed, but I wanted to understand God, and they were there to explain Him. I was born the family sponge. My father would rephrase this as "squeaky wheel" because I had an endless string of questions forming in my head, but I put everything towards the pursuit of knowing God, and I absorbed every word they said.

In high school, I was your go-to-Christian-friend. I carried my Bible to school everyday, and slept with it under my pillow at night. Sophomore year, I was elected president of the Fellowship of Christian athletes – leading bible study twice a week before class.

By the second semester in college, I'd taken a leadership position at the BSU (Baptist Student Union) – teaching bible studies in dorm rooms, praying with my friends through their biology exams, and driving my peers across the state to various Christian conferences and retreats.

This is when I found my exit door. These conferences were designed to inspire young people to "Go" (in other words, find some place to evangelize). And I'd long since been wanting to go, largely because I chose to believe that Southern Baptist theology was the only truth, and I didn't want anyone to go to hell. I see now, it's because I love people.

But also because somewhere deep inside of me, I knew I couldn't stay in Mississippi. So I went. Every school break we had, I went to any place they would send me and I did the work they asked of me.

By senior year, I'd developed a plan to move to Hamilton, Ontario to work for a Southern Baptist church planting network that I'd interned at the previous summer

—in the name of Jesus, in pursuit of my father's pride, and from as far a distance as possible.

I'm grateful that you're holding this book in your hands.
Regardless of the reason.

-Bugg

My Father is a Pastor.

My Father is a Capricorn.

My Father is SATURN.

On the day you are born, Saturn is in the room,
observing from a very specific position.

He is the Father figure in astrology,
bringing structure and rules, indifferent about comfort.

He establishes your foundation.
He gives you a blueprint.

Through childhood, he is the shadow on your heels,
watching to see what you build with what you've been handed.

PART 01

(Genesis 1:1-5)

THE INHERITANCE

In the Beginning

It's Day 1.

You are a thread in the void—
an idea swimming inside the mind of God.

You are hidden,
in the darkness you haven't been told to run from yet.

You are asleep,
under the light you haven't been told to hide from yet.

Things You Should Know About My Father

1. My Father is a Pastor
2. He always works on Easter.
3. He loves God more than anything.
4. **He loves his family.**
5. He loves cornbread and fried fish.
6. He is a fisherman.
7. He is a fisher of men
8. He loves football.
9. He loves a game night.
10. He loves to win.
11. **He loves his family.**
12. He taught his daughters how to win.
13. He is a Capricorn.
14. He doesn't believe in astrology.
15. He believes in the 2nd amendment.
16. He believes in protecting those he loves.
17. He believes in Salvation through the blood of Jesus Christ.
18. He is proud to be an American.
19. He is proud to be a child of God
20. [I hope] He is proud to be my father.
21. **He loves his family.**

Irish Twins

I close my eyes and wake up at 5am
in the fall of 2003.
We jog to the end of a gravel road
and catch the bus for school.

      We're in the aisle,
      fighting over who gets to sit by the window.
      Some call this sibling discord,
      but we're the kinda kids that'll flip a coin
      and honor fate.

I close my eyes and wake up at 8 years old.
I break one of Momma's vases.
My sister is 10 and she teaches me,

      what they don't know, can't hurt 'em.

      She was born resourceful.
      I was born naïve.
      She could see through dust –
      taught me to squint my eyes
      when it hurts to take a closer look.

I close my eyes and wake up to my father
yelling – like
if we breathe too loud, we lose
our toys, which is all we have to distract ourselves
inside this black hole, in Black Water Creek.

      If they take our toys, we have to return

to watching grass grow or making mud pies and
pretending to feed them to Grandma.

This is not a form of revenge –
it's just the sound of a jukebox blaring
in an empty fish house, on a backroad in Mississippi,   or
a way out of hearing Momma cry again –
as we dance barefoot in the trees.

It's avoiding the weight of an emotional responsibility
that was never ours to carry.
But in the middle of nowhere,
who else will?

My Father Nicknamed Me Motor Mouth

I got feelings that exit my body through the mouth.

Speed of speech transforms my hot wheels into
a NASCAR race, and I'm hiding my secrets beneath bathwater.

I'm 12, still taking toys into the tub,
talking to the wall outlets like they are the ears of God,
and caking bubbles on my face to seem more masculine
because I really need Him to hear me.

The Pastor's Daughter

The golden child on display.
Can he see,

me?

The Real Junk Yard Goats

If you made me pick favorites,
I'd choose my father first,
but I'd never tell him
because he's a Capricorn.

You can't tell a Capricorn things like this.

I learned what you can't tell a Capricorn
from my sister, who is a Capricorn;
my sister, who was molded from a rib
ripped from my father's side
on his 24th birthday.

I admit, at times
I am jealous of what they share;
of a certainty they don't have to try for
because they were born with it.

I confess, at times
I envy how the teeth marks
on their demons' arms
echo the bark bursting from their chests.

Twins from a past life—back together—
pushing against the walls closing in,
pushing a world of people towards the truth.

People Pleasers Cry in Private

I got feelings that exit my body through the eyes.

Think, bloodshot, and
snot dripping from the tip of the nose,
and emotions I don't know the name of yet.
I let it puddle onto the floor & drag out the mop.

Because I've seen what happens
when you don't clean up your messes –
the way they notice
but not in the way you want them to,
and then comes the impulsive knee-jerk-need
to explain yourself,
as you fixate on fixing your mistakes
so they don't look at you like you're helpless.

Sunday Potlucks

There are questions
cooked into the cornbread,
that we avoid.
Is it the crumbs,
caught in the corners of our mouths,
stopping us just shy of asking?

We wipe buttery residue from our lips with our elbows
and draw out a thank you that makes the magnolias sing.

Maybe it's the way stain glass Jesus stares at us
as we break bread,
that makes me wonder why,
even if we're already stuffed,
we follow the demands of our southern charm
when the next course arrives:

> *"Yes ma'am I'll have the mashed potatoes,"* and
> *"Yes sir I'll have some collard greens"* and
> *"Yes ma'am I'll have a hushpuppy"* and
> *"Yes sir I'll have the ham hock and white beans".*

Those elusive questions
climb to the tips of our tongues and slip out,
make it halfway across the table,
and are silenced by a bottle of Tabasco;

So by the time we're drowning the fried catfish in hot sauce, we've all
    forgotten the passage from the sermon,
      forgiven the pastor for preaching 3 minutes past noon,
      and gulped down the questions entirely for the promise of

dessert.

Then the proof comes in the banana pudding,
shovelled onto styrofoam plates,
as the wonders we wished we'd said,
slosh around in our bellies.

But maybe it's the way we all sigh in unison,
as we pack up leftovers like the Fish and Loaves miracle;
maybe it's knowing deep down the path to the heart
is always through the stomach;
maybe it's the Sunday potlucks that make me believe,
there's always a reason to come back to the table.

"Yes ma'am, I'll have another piece of cornbread"

Preteen Prayer Closet

I told God the secrets I couldn't tell my dad.
       like, my first crush on a girl two pews behind us.

I'd go in my closet every morning to pray for her.
I'd wave at her on Sundays. trying
not to blush.

Then someone said God sends gay people to hell.
So, I went back in my closet and told God I was kidding.
I looked in the mirror and told myself that too.

Game Night

Wanting to win and lose at the same time is the same as
wanting to make Daddy proud but be nothing like him.

Or the same as loving to watch him pout when you beat him,
and trying not to cry when he beats you.

If you win, he calls you a cheater.
You laugh like a disney villain.
You serve him his own medicine and that's justice,
                                    or feels like it.

But that "good" feeling dissolves like a
communion cracker on your tongue, when you look
in the mirror and resent yourself
because you cannot deny the resemblance.

You, looking at yourself look just like him,
while you play Monopoly with your friends.

Fish Hook

I found a fish hook in my throat from the year 2000,
        from the year my daddy came home from walmart
        with a "push-to-cast" pink, Barbie rod.

        We went to the pond and caught crappie all afternoon.

        Every time I had the strength to reel them in myself,
        my father's eyes became gold star stickers, stuck to my face.

I wore those trophies on my cheeks for years to come.

        until I realized I didn't want to fish anymore;
        until I admitted I was no fisher of men;
        until I confessed that baiting & casting & catching & reeling
        and killing & cleaning carcasses
        was not my calling.

        And those gold stars lost their adhesive almost as quickly as my
        father's face turned.

There's this fish hook stuck in my throat,
and I can't figure out
        how to get it loose;
        how to untangle the line that leads back to that hillside in
        Mississippi;
        how to make our differences make sense, when we look just
        alike;
        how to even begin to talk about it.

There's a fish hook that digs a hole into my lung

when I have to make eye contact with him.
     I can't breathe from the fear of letting him down.

     I can't breathe from the panic in me
     to jump off the line and swim away.

Sounds You Got Mud in the Veins

This is the ground on which grief turns away
from cartoon cucumbers losing their hair brushes;
from the innocence of misunderstanding
the talking tomato's intentions;
grief is screaming,

this—is not fiction.

This—is an impenetrable fear of "other",
where women raise their pitchforks of tolerance
and bear the cross of concern in your honor.
Their prayers are branded into their knees.
They are begging God to make you
turn from your heathen ways.

This, is where the kids with the wrong questions
get buried beneath boots,
under foot stomping worship,
as we raise our voices louder,
hoping God hears and is proud.

This is the ground where trust never grows,
rotten soil, from dead bodies
left laying—their roots
tangled up in our bones,
while we argue over which brand of communion crackers
Jesus wants us to use or
whether or not our gay cousin
will burn in hell.

Sinners' Whip

I'm never innocent and you can tell
by the way I'm crying
before you've gotten to the edge of the bed,
to tell me you wish you didn't have to do this.
But you do this because *this* is love.

You look sad as you pick the belt out.

You look like you've been given a message from God
to take your daughter up a mountain and burn her alive.

You look disappointed to me.

Are you disappointed in me?

is all I can think about,
as my sternum digs into my chest, trying to pull up the words
I'm sorry.
I'm sorry. I'm sorry. I'm sorry, Daddy.
I'm always so sorry.
Because I'm never innocent.
Because I was born into sin.
Because I have been talking back
to the demons in my closet
everytime God turns his head.

Tunnel Vision

I want my life to make sense, so I listen for someone to talk some into
me.

Every sermon I've ever heard telling me to pray,
is an American diploma in my hands.

Every sermon I've ever heard telling me to give,
is a white robe draped over my shoulders.

Every sermon I've ever heard telling me to go,
is the pomp and circumstance beneath my feet.

I've been waiting forever to get out of Mississippi.
I've been praying forever to get out of Mississippi.

I'm throwing my cap in the air, and leaving to share the good news,

you can get out of Mississippi.

The Gun

I graduated and Daddy bought me a gun.
For a year, I owned a gun
and I never shot it.
I was too busy packing my bags.
I was too busy, so

I placed my pistol
in the hands of my pastor,
which is to say my father.
I told him he could have it back.

I thought I didn't need it where I was going.
And he's the one who earned the dollar
to give us the chance,
to own a gun.

He's the one
who paid the price
at the counter,
at graduation, so
I left it.

I ran away from my father,
which is to say, my gun.

To My Pastor

Dear Dad,

I didn't mean to bury myself beneath trying so hard not to mess up.
I just wanted you to be proud of me.

Church

You have your hands in the pocket of your slacks while Miss G plays
the piano.

Amazing Grace.

You sing loud enough that it counts towards your crown but not as loud
as you would in the shower.

The shower is the altar where true worshippers lay their bodies and
heave; their tears mirroring the faucet; grief & shame spewing out;
repentance happens here. Dove soap washing you of conviction, naked
before the God of the universe. Do you feel shame at the thought of
that, like Adam, or Eve, or Jonah or Judas?

Is it because you feel the innate need to be private about what's going
on in your body? Is privacy a part of obedience? Tell me, any of you –
show me the book, the verse, the letters dipped in crimson red.

Can I dance naked before the Lord and be blessed, like David? Is David
someone to admire? The coloring sheets from childhood sing *AMEN*,
but your face changes when I square him up to things I've yet to confess.

At the End of the Sermon

They call Miss G to the piano.
The pastor's conclusion is always the same:

> *"Do you know,*
> > *that you know,*
> > > *that you know,*

"that Jesus is your savior and Lord?"

One of a thousand repeated phrases,
hammered like iron nails
into the tracks in my brain.

The truth is, I've never *known* anything with that kind of confidence.

But for a woman of God, confidence isn't necessary.
For a woman of God, the path to salvation is through submission,
through blind faith, for lifting the broom, stirring the pot,
and raising the little ones to trust and obey.

Emotional Intelligence

[as the title of a really difficult video game]

Contrary to previous beliefs,
apologizing isn't a social skill.
It's an emotional one:

Birth is level 1 - *the first cry* -
one of the few that no one tells us to stop.   Then, they do.

Level 2 is where we learn to say it to ourselves.

Level 3 is where we stare in a mirror crying.

Level 4 is where we stare in a mirror crying saying stop.
                                                        stop. stop!

Level 5 is where we stare in a mirror having pressed the dissociation
powerup button;
                        the cool down for that one is some dial up BS.

Level 6 is where our father tells us to stop crying because,
        "I brought you into this world and I can take you out of it"
        "because if you don't stop, I'll give you something to cry about"
        "because in Mississippi, we throw some dirt on it and move on."

Level 7 is not crying in the dugout after we strike out.

Level 8 is tuning out our father's voice at the next at bat.

Level 9 is an unwashed pillow caked in dried snot.

Level 10 is a pair of fake glasses from Claire's to hide swollen eyes.

Level 11 is "don't embarrass me in public with all that whining".

Level 12-50 is the soul numbness comparative of a tingly ass after sitting in a mildew seeped pew for hours.

Level 51-90 is the first, and then many, therapy sessions in the daunting age of adulthood and in the hidden looming presence of Saturn's return.

Level 91 is apologizing to our families, our friends, our pets, our coworkers, and every stranger that looks at us for too long.

Level 92-98 is sleepless night after sleepless night, going back to the mirror, crying but not saying stop, handing ourselves a tissue as an act of compassion, whispering the word *valid* not because it's a social media trend but because we actually want to mean it.

Level 99 is the apology we say to the child that's been wailing inside of us since we left the womb, turns to a whimper that drifts softly into forgiveness.

The video game tutorial is now complete.

♄

We run from the pressure of our father but still,
it follows.

It is said in astrology, that approximately every 29 years,
Saturn returns to the position he occupied at your birth.

They say this "return" marks your real adulthood,
when you reckon with who you were told to be,
and are faced with who you truly are.

Everything you've come to know, every belief
you've acquired or created since the beginning,
is up for review.

Part Two

(Genesis 1:6-31)

The Creation

Spotlights & Performance —

Notes from the Pastor's Youngest

You'd think that I got addicted to attention
the minute they shined that light in my face,
hands balled up into fists,
bloody, naked, and crying.

It was a set up.
Staged.
A full production.
At the foot of a hospital bed,

All eyes on me, as I come out
into the world you are living in.
I don't remember feeling it
but I *know* the feeling —

       the eyes of God always watching over me,
       me, always watching over my shoulder
       to make sure I'm doing a good job.

I *know* the feeling
of eyes on the body,
the body not knowing how to respond.
I know the shiver that exposure sends
through the nervous system.

The feeling like you're looking at me
but right now I'm a mess
and I don't want you to see.

But then the feeling, *after* the feeling

The feeling I was born to bleed
in front of you,
to cry on your couches,
get snot on your pillows,
stand naked,
and not run away.

If I'm going to show you the truth
about who I am,
then it must be a full production.
 Must be stylized,
 must be big,
 must be real,
 must be beautiful,
 must be dressed in costumes,
  draped in symbols
  leaking with meaning.
  A full production.

I want God seated
in a box with the best view.
I want the spotlight
shining into eyes that make you believe
they don't know how to open yet.

I want Saturn holding my mother's hand
as she pushes me into center stage,
 face purple from holding my breath,
  crying,
  screaming,
  wailing from the chest,
  I want Saturn to hold *me.*

I want Saturn to hold me.

I Got the Job

I'm an interview ace, answering your questions
with questions, just like Jesus.

Just like Jesus, I embrace the hand you offer, I sit
attentive, I make prolonged eye contact
to show you I'm listening.

I'm listening. I've always been listening
to your instructions on what makes me good,
to your suggestions on what could make me better.

What could make me better?
Because I still don't feel good enough.

But Daddy, I got a job at a church, and I'm moving
to Canada to share the good news.

The good news, that there is a place we can go,
besides here.

Self Denial Makes Me Sick

I'm folding an American flag like it's a funeral,
planting it in the community garden to see what grows—
who knows?

Blind faith is a kind of wide-eyed wonder
and even an empty sky is beautiful if you've been in the dark awhile.

I stand up straight and salute my sense of grief and my grandma
during the general inspection of my first Canadian apartment.

I march the hallways with a mop, & do extra push ups to prove a point.
I've been trained for war but still, I run away from it.

I want to linger at the edges, make the bed, make small talk,
make excuses for why I'm not ready. Make the house look real pretty.

But Grandma is gone and silence is spoon feeding fear for breakfast,
making me run laps when I refuse. I vomit it all over my shoes.

The Tower in Reverse

I inherited my father's legos when I was 10,
       Granny found them in the back of a closet,
       said they'd be worth some money,

       as if I'd sell the devil his legos back,
       as if I'd ever hand over my paths to escape,
       as if I didn't take seriously the potential of building with
plastic.

I labeled every lego
       by length
       and width
       and I went to work.

I built a world
to earn the stamp of my father's approval,
       and then I built another
       and another
       and another.

       World after world,
       I built out of legos,
       I built in my head,
       I built a wall around my ego.
       I built to prove something or
           to prove someone wrong.

I built a tower out of my father's legos
with only two ways down:
       jump
      or   f
           a
            \
             /

Monotony

The church bell is singing loudly,
on a walk down Locke St. in February.
The wind stirs, the cold burns, the gray covers,
and the church bell is growing louder.

A lady runs in heels, towards the entrance
to the fellowship hall, before the service,
a dog barks at a brick wall that doesn't respond,
the winter is a nine-tail whip, aimed at my face, and

the church bell is inside of me, ringing
in my ears, reminding me it's time
for the lesson, it's time to come near, come in,
come out of the cold, and I do

because the church bell is inside of me.
Commanding, inside of me,
demanding, inside of me,
an auditory avalanche;

I am buried inside of me.

Near the Door

On Sundays, I prefer the work.

> I prefer the predictable to-do-list,
> laid out on the altar by women for centuries.
> I prefer the pastor's teachings while I'm on my feet,
> so I can rock back and forth, prepared
> to meet the needs of the congregation.

On Sundays, I prefer the outskirts.

> I prefer a wall to lean on, where I can watch and wonder
> what God thinks of it all.
> I prefer to stand by the exits, or near the bathroom,
> where I can escape, and hide, and pray
> for God to speak.

On Sundays, I prefer the thresholds.

> I prefer the introductions and the conclusions,
> and watching the sanctuary's energy shift,
> and writing my doubts between the lines in my Bible.
> I prefer keeping those to myself.

On Sundays, I prefer the youth.

> I prefer their openness and their honesty
> and the innocence in their uncertainty,
> and the way faith feels alive when *they* wonder.
> I prefer how much easier it is to stomach,
> when the questions are coming from them.

Holy Avoidance

Ode to the THF Youth Group

The first day I sat with you,
we read together, Genesis.
A beginning.

> We question how a garden can be perfect,
> about what it means to plant an idea in the ground
> and watch it grow.

I start you off with this: *why?*

> *Why* this seed and not that one?
> *Why* apples instead of oranges?
> Why *don't we*   or why *do we*
> bite the fruit that promises realization?

Why   is the question you ask
before you learn the answers you seek
are within your own body.

You all sat cross legged and attentive in grass
that would soon be washed in snow.
You looked at me as if I had the answers,
but we were not separate from one another
in our curiosity for God.
So we tore through the pages
of creation and I asked you:

> *How can* a seed of free thought survive the winter here?

> How can I teach you that faith is a choice?

How do I help you through the wilderness of blind beliefs?

It's *your* salvation to work out.
Whether in fear and trembling
or in an invigorating awe and wonder.

Just ask why.

[breathe]

I catch myself thinking of my parents,
of how precisely I've mimicked their footsteps.
And I ask myself   why
it feels selfish to know they brag of me.
There's a tomb of trophies inside my chest
from how well I've followed instructions and

my heart is on my sleeve for all of you to see,
torn between burying my own doubts
and answering yours honestly.

You ask me questions and when I don't answer,
you ask one another.
This is always the better solution.

I remember the day you asked how God felt about queerness.
I mimed Jesus by answering you with a question.

What do *you* think?

You all answered together
by planting a mustard seed in the cold ground beneath your feet.

I Have a Confession

The coffee is helping.
I prefer it in a mug because it's familiar.

.

The handle is a seat belt for my fingers, that would otherwise
tear apart the tissue box on my therapist's desk.

.

Anxiety thrives in our extremities. That's what she's saying.
To make me feel better. I appreciate the help
even though it isn't helping.

.

The coffee is helping.
The thing keeping me from putting my hand over my mouth.
The thing holding space for me to say it.

.

I'm safe here, so I'm about to say it.

.

I'm almost 25 so it's time I say it.

.

.

I say, *I'm about to say it.*

.

.

.

She says to say it.

.

.

.

I say, *I'm gonna say it —*

The Pastor Fired Me

"He's probably protecting his reputation."

Fuck your reputation.

It took me 'till the bottom of the bottle
to get the message,
that you are bottom of the barrel –

to figure out I was the trigger
on the gun
aimed at my own head.

I'm dead in a bed
that I made,
bowing to men who bow to money and control.

Tough lessons learned
through taking the long way.

I bloomed late, like your facial hair—
half-grown soul patch,
crumb catcher
saving everything for later.

You – Judas Iscariot,
Shepherd of nothing.

You are the one who left the table early.

You are nothing like my father.
You are half-cooked. Clown looking. Coward.
Lazy in your convictions—
eating out of hands, that keep a knife near your throat—
making deals with a different kind of devil—

slaughtering your sheep.

We are just bodies to burn;
fuel on the altar of your ego,

as you carve the pipeline beneath your castle.

80k a year and you get to hibernate for most of it. But
they're watching you –
like you were watching me,
even though you still failed to see
until I told you.

So I've told you.
And now I tell the world.

just because you have
a degree in theology, doesn't give you
sole authority
on who God is. You are
not a powerful man.

Daddy, I'm Dating a Scorpio; Pray for Me

a letter of confession I don't have the guts to send

Dear Daddy, Canada is cold these days. I know I haven't written in a while, but there's some things going on that I can't tell you. Firstly, the church is fighting. We don't seem to agree on what the word *integrity* means. It's difficult to put into words at this time. There's a leadership meeting on Tuesday. I'll know more then.

I just want you to know I haven't given up. I'm trying. You know me, I'm a trier. But I'm tired, if I'm being honest with you. Tired of these people who seem to care more about their reputations than they do the Gospel. I've been thinking a lot about Jesus lately. I've noticed some things that I hadn't before, like the way He shows up in unexpected places. At a random Starbucks, for example, where they turn water into coffee and coffee into honest friendship. Or on the Italian widow's front porch next door, in the peak of Covid isolation. Or in a laundromat, where a bunch of poets gather to collect tears and wash feet.

You know where I've seen him the least these days? —

Anyway, things are changing, and I'm scared to tell you. If I were to tell you what I wanted to tell you, I wouldn't tell you I'm gay. I would tell you that I've met a woman that I've fallen in love with. I'd tell you she's a Scorpio, and I'd laugh, but you wouldn't because you wouldn't get it and that's okay. But then, I'd tell you that means that she's got a heart the size of the ocean and it doesn't always fit inside of her body. I'd tell you she is unwaveringly loyal to the people she chooses to love, I'd tell you a story to contextualize it, I'd say:

Daddy, you wouldn't believe this, but the other day, after all the bullshit went down at church, my girlfriend ripped a painting off the wall [that was given to her by the pastor's daughter] and returned it to her doorstep, with a letter quoting Corinthians, which led to all of us getting blocked on social media

She's got Peter's sword on her hip, doesn't she? Paul would hate her. You wouldn't. She's a fighter; and that's what love takes, right? I know this from you. From our family. From getting it wrong over and over, but getting up somehow and trying again. It's in our blood. It's in hers too. We're not as different as you think. We're not as different as I once thought.

Things are changing, and I hope it's for the better. I wish I could tell you these things. But I can't. So I'll tell you I quit. I'll tell you that things are pretty good. They're just changing. Lots of changes.

I wish I could tell you these things.

September

is for the sad bois
that come out at sunset
when silence sinks below the horizon
into a Sunday,
and snooze gets hit on the reminder
to visit your nearest sanctuary.

Last week, somebody read me the statements
of the satanic faith and
I sobbed. Because why do they seem
to be more like Jesus than the saints.

Saints, tell me,
why you have been wearing masks
long before Covid set in,
then refuse to wear masks
to prove a power point in a pandemic.

Going to church now is like drinking wine
laced with a virus for the soul.
My chest is aching from the gift of solitude

given to me graciously via social
media blocking and silent treatments
and you, looking over your shoulder when you
see me on the street,
pretending I am not, and never was, at your service
since the 19th day of September
some long time ago.

"Integrity issues" is the stamp on the stomach of my poster child shirt,
the thorn you stabbed into my side,
to help me remember that straying
into any conflicting thought what-so-ever
means being kicked off the island.

Returning to the flock requires picking up
the old, dusty cross of your delusional reality
and dragging it uphill.

And so long as I abide in your statues,
I shall survive the scrutiny of an entire community of people
that call themselves Southern Baptists.

Tell me, does Jesus save you
an extra fancy space behind those pearly gates
because you're serious about conversion therapy,
and salvation through repentance
of the sins that you've translated yourself from Hebrew and Greek,
and stale crackers at communion, and the color of the carpet?

Or will it be that Heaven is just like September here,
when the weather could go either way,
and everyone is going back to school,
and pastors are writing sermons last minute
because they were too busy watching sports,
and everyone has the same shot at waking up the next day
to take a deep breath, and see the sun rise?

Self Pity

I'm a cake-eater, a people pleaser,
I'm bright-eyed and bushy-tailed,
I'm the extra vanilla creamer in Momma's coffee
I am a 15 year old sweet tooth
       cavity, grounded from the cookie jar.

I'm anxious,
I'm an overused corn-bred recipe,
I'm a task-list enthusiast,
I am the queer-rotten-apple
       of my daddy's eye; he's lost his glasses.

I'm the daughter of lower,
       middle class parents,
       in the land of private health care.
I'm a scarlet fever sneeze,
I'm ADHD, at the back of the medicine cabinet,
I am the waterboarded lungs of pneumonia; screaming.

I'm restless,
I'm a leg, rattling the economy seats,
I'm 3 cigarettes a day,
I am the middle finger on the hand
       of a 23 year old, leaving Mississippi.

I'm eager to please; to watch
       Crave at the end of the day,
       dim-eyed and flat-lined,
I'm a worn-out Star Wars t-shirt,
I'm the ex-church poster child,
I am the beaver who gave a dam
             and *d r o w n e d .*

I'm Not Defensive, but I am a Leo Moon

Let me tell you, for the sake of saying it;
I don't care if you unfollow me.

Let me tell you, *for the sake of reminding myself,*
I don't care if you dislike my choices.
I don't care if you want to slide into the cold green lake of my DMs
to explain what your opinion of God's opinion on my opinion of God is.

Let me tell you, so you don't feel obligated to waste your energy.
I don't care if you feel religious responsibility
to take me on a journey of your understanding
of the prodigal son
who returns for the fatted calf laid out on a hot fire
by their earthly father.

Tell my father I'm vegetarian with a side of bacon
—if you feel the absolute need to get involved.
Tell him I'm not coming home to his religious grandeur
where men tack up their shadows on women's shoulders
while they do the dishes, after a long ass shift at work.

Let me tell you—for you and the rest of the universe to hear—
so you don't get upset when I don't respond,
—or I do respond
and tell you
          to fuck off.

I don't care that I don't believe in your version of God anymore,
and I don't care that the only way to your cushy afterlife is through
sitting in the same pew for decades,
listening to the same 10 sermons on rotation,

pretending at the potluck that you listened.

I don't care that the river of milk and honey is in your koolaid pitcher
because you open up a 1000 page book every day
and bruise your knees on your suburban carpet,
begging God to change his mind about queer people's DNA.

Drink up.
Drink that Koolaid dry
and feel the joy of the Lord as your strength.
Because I don't care.

Saturn's Last Call

He's never cared for excuses,
and I'm late. But I want to explain,
      it's *because* last night,

    I was at the bar.
    I was busy living.

    I was "head in the game"
      or"head in the ass",
          face in the glass,
          facing the fact
          that he always acts like a period;
          like a grumpy bartender,
          closing the curtains,
          sending us home,
          when we're not finished—

    he cuts me off, mid sentence.
    Because it's time to leave, but
    I'm leaning in against the edge of the bar
    hoping it wedges itself between my ribs;

a kind of self-inflicted thorn,
a kind of "I'm avoiding tomorrow" and I'll pay for it.
a kind of "can I get one more" and then the bill.

I'm out of shape;
    out of sorts,

out of touch,
out of my mind,

  procrastinating
    o n   a l l   t h e   t h i n g s
  that are mine to fix,
  like:

the dishwasher that's been broken for 6 months
  (excuse)

the pile of parking tickets I have to pay
  (excuse)

the empty egg carton in the fridge
  (excuse)

the *truth*, I'm running out of time to own up to my life.

My Last Prayer

Delilah asked Sampson 3 times.
"Where does your power come from?"

I'm leaning against the pillars of my life, I've cut my own hair off. I've cut my own family off. I've auctioned my abilities off to the highest bidders—to the ones offering sugar-coated applause for the power I bring to the table—to the ones that would use me. Use me. Use me. Love me. Please use me if you'll love me. Please love me. Look at all the things I can do.

I'm leaning against the pillars of my life, blind, in a foreign land, in a room full of people whose voices I've memorized and recognize by the sentiments they use over and over. Now, every move I make is being questioned by the pastor, the deacons, their wives, and their children. I've spilled my guts out on the floor for them; I've gouged my own eyes out, to prove my belief in a God we cannot see. I know I'm not one of you, but I believe.

I'm leaning against the pillars of my life, when I smell the blood. When I realize it's on my hands. When I understand, for the first time, that this place isn't holy, it's hollow with shame. And I'm leaning over the edge, when I recognize I don't belong here.

I'm pushing
against the pillars of my life,
begging God to give me back my power
just long enough
to make the walls crumble.

To My Capricorn

Dear Dad,

I would never lie to you
without lying to myself first.
With the mirror you gave me,
I turn every page, analyze every edge,

paper cut scars to prove it,
on the wrists—
or the center of the palms;
I know we argue about where the nails went.

Why are you looking at me that way?
I didn't lie.
I didn't lie to you.
I lied to myself.
I survived.
I hid the feelings between the lines,
and whispered it in my sleep
to the wind chimes.

I would never lie to you.
Look me in the eye.

The Delta Blues

at a bar in Elora, Ontario

No one smokes cigarettes in Elora.
I don't smoke cigarettes.
But I'm standing on the front porch of a bar
1000 miles north of the Mason Dixon,
smoking my way through a whole pack.

Inside, there's a girl playing a harmonica, and
it sounds like the South singing me a pecan-pie-lullaby.
But sweet as the South can sound sometimes, I can't sleep
because I thought I'd never miss you but I do.

And I guess that's what happens
when you notice a detail you didn't see before,
like the way two or three freckles align
like constellations on the face.

You didn't use to strike me as something to pay attention to.
I'd stare out your window every day dreaming of another life.
In my head, you used to be a man with a beard
down to his knees, asking women to worship with a comb,
but I was a kid who played with scissors
and we didn't— couldn't —find the middle ground.
You used to be old and privileged and too hardened to understand,
demanding your opinions to be written into history and science;

I grew bored of you,

telling me to listen to the birds and watch the grass grow,
insisting there was something to learn from it.
I resented you, for the ways you confined me.

These days though, something is changing.
You're more like a young lady; a voice like butter, dressed in all black
the skeletons in your closet have crafted symphonies
that have reached out of you and cradled the earth
in a melancholy understanding.

You're the most sad, most angry, most confused woman I've ever seen,
and it bleeds out onto canvas,
even when you try to hide it behind hymns and hospitality.
Looking at you now, I see myself,
crying through my last cigarette,
the taste of Mississippi on my tongue,
missing home.

I Fired the Pastor

After I lost my job, I called my father to let him know
I would no longer be working for the church,
in pursuit of opening a coffee shop.

This was not a lie.
It was truth told from an overcrowded elevator, closing in my head.

I called my father to let him know life was turning
faster than I could run,
but I was rolling with the punches.

This was not a lie.
It was truth told from an overcrowded elevator, going down in my head.

I called my father to let him know I'd been thinking about him a lot,
that I appreciated him being my pastor all these years,
but I was ready for him to be my dad again.

This was not a lie.
It was the open, empty truth.

I've Always Had to Work on Easter

This year I'm behind a bar on a Thursday.
Every seat was warm until midnight.

Sloppy slurs spill from the mouth, the subconscious longing
for Friday to be the kind of "good" they say it is:

      Ask all the other Fridays how they feel about the "good" one
            and they'll nail it to a cross for being different.

Good Friday shows up to meet us in the middle
      —between delusions and truth—

      granting half of society permission
            to drop their burdens for one extra day and get a drink.
      The rest of us will be behind a bar
            to pick up what they're laying down.

Then it's 1am and the bar is a tomb.

We draw curtains, queue songs, pour post-shift beers.
We discuss death like he's a regular we can't figure out.

Then it's 1:30 and our drinks are almost finished.

Someone tells me they envy my faith, which feels ironic,
      but I think even Jesus looked around once in a awhile
        and wondered if any of it mattered.

◆

I smoke a joint in the empty street after we leave,
       I think of Gethsemane,
       of the way Thursday must've felt on the shoulders of the Son
       of God.

       Friday was just "tomorrow" back then,
          as beads of blood formed on his brow
          while he begged to flex the plan.

"If there's any other way to do this…"

Yet we all know, whether we are God or not,
       responsibilities will show up to arrest us,
       to escort us away from our metaphors and fantasies.

Tabs must be paid; and the whole world is on the hunt
for some form of salvation.

The Burning Bush is Saturn

The bush is on fire.
I attempt to speak with it.
But communication is nature's poker game,
so there are stakes.

I search my pants for chips to contribute.
But there's a hole in my pocket I didn't notice until now.

> *My pocket turns itself inside out*
> *and makes a scene out of its own emptiness.*
> *My face turns red;*
> *I blame it on the heat.*

The bush is on fire.
It's hard to talk to.
But I finally found a chip.
It's on my shoulder.

I peel it off and try to place a bet,
but the bush doesn't accept
things coated in sugar.

So I eat it instead.
It tastes like a chocolate covered ego.
It lands like a joke in my stomach.

> *My stomach turns itself inside out*
> *and makes a scene out of its own emptiness,*
> *growling for something of substance;*
> *I blame it on the sugar.*

The bush is, somehow still, **on fire.**
and instead of explaining myself, finally I

just watch it burn.

Question from the Bottom

How many times?

How many times
does it have to crash and burn
to ashes that you pour
into the lake of tears
you dug long ago,
somewhere in Mississippi.

How many times do you have to start over?

How many times
does your head
have to hit the door frame
       you didn't see coming even though
it's smacked you between the eyes
1000 times before.

How many times
will you bank on the idea of "eternity"
and scour the earth in search of
something or someone
to dissolve yourself into,
to feel alive in this reality.

How many times will you have to start over?

How many times
will Saturn smash
those rose-colored glasses
to shards; the ones hanging on your face
by the same strand of duct tape

you've been using to fix everything.

How many times
will you use a bandaid
where a bonfire is needed?

How many times will you return
to your knees, to scrub the feet
of people who've walked all over you.

How many times will you forget
the lessons that Daddy preached,
written on the walls in your chest—
every verse
you hid in your heart, neatly
painted over every secret
you refused to tell
about yourself.

How many times
will you pace the hallways
in your body,
trying to translate the language
between you and your demons;
trying not to misrepresent
the narrative you inherited;
trying not to betray yourself.

How many times
will you overthink this?

Shotgun with Shelby

I'm in the front seat crying over my first break up,
crying over what to do with the cats
or the dog or the plants or the books or the art
or the records or the memories that have rooted
themselves into a jungle of life
in five years' time. I'm attached.
And I'm blind in the eye
of a storm I called for.

I'm in the front seat crying over
the way I left,
the love of my life,
the comfort of community—
      a wonderland,
      a perfect, polaroid-able dream
      we drew up together
      between the sheets
      of each others' innocence.

It was in her arms,
I woke up safe enough
to grow again.
And so I grew again.   I grew and
grew and grew into the realizations, like

      I'm still just a kid.
      and I've just arrived inside
      this holy chapter of humanity;
      and now, I know.
           I know,
                that I know,
                  that I know,

                              almost nothing—

                              about what I want;
                              about who I am.

I'm in the front seat crying,
because I feel it all, all at once
and I take a pill
so I'll feel nothing,
but right now,   I   feel   everything.
I feel glued inside a nightmare.
I feel the tunnel caving in,
I feel ready to die,
          and then, Saturn,

grabbing my hand.
Telling me to cry, and
turning up the music
that hurts so good,
and hurts so bad,
and hurts like the first wound
that never did get kissed,
and hurts like the first time,
and every time
you remember leaving.

I'm in the front seat crying
because I'm leaving.
Because I have to go back,
I have to trace my steps
and trace the threads
leading back to my body.

I'm in the front seat crying
over all that has fallen
          in on me;
          around me;

because of me;

I'm in the front seat,
gripping the dash, heaving
over what I know
is still left to burn.

I'm in the front seat, and
Saturn's rings surround me,
reminding me
that comfort isn't a sin,
that the xanax will kick in,
but until then,

she's holding my hand,
and it's the only thing helping.

Breathe.

Thunder & Lightning Usher You Home

Everytime you smell magnolias, what you're smelling is a memory.
Close your eyes and point

> to   the sticky putty carpet stain,
> the hole in the wall,
> the boy's arm that you broke at church,
> the glass of iced tea you spilled at the fish house,
> the tomato soup left burning on the stove,
> the dinner plate you broke,
> the rips in your clothes,
> the missing binding of your books,
> the ink all over your arms and hands,
> the paper scattered around your room.

Everytime you hear the wind chimes, it's your ancestors playing hide
and seek. You'll learn in time,

> they are a clever gang, difficult to pen down
> all at once, but they'll pass you their magic
> in fragments, on chipped china
> pulled from the cabinet for special occasions.

It'll be a curious thing   when you cut your finger for the first time,
> get your first scar,
>> your first whooping,
>> your first bible,
>> your first pen,
>> your first journal,
>> your first car,
>> your first doorway out.

Your ancestors are present. You can hear them speaking, when you are
too.

They can teach you things, like
        how compassion smells like the earth just before it rains,
        and it thunders for people who are watching

            their mother cry again,
                as grandma tries to change the subject,
                and grandaddy snores in harmony
                with the wind chimes swinging on the porch.

            There's a storm coming.

            Can you smell the magnolias?

Late, Again

You blame them all at least once
for one thing or another,
at some point in time.

Sometimes you even point at time
as the suspect
in every scene,
where projections of perfection
cast onscreen
—glitch.

The timing was off.
The timing wasn't right.
Too early.
Too late.
Tomorrow,
I'll stop the watch,
and count on my fingers
to hold it all together,
to keep time
in line
where it's supposed to be.

Where are you supposed to be?

Time doesn't care.
You do.
You choose.

The timing can't be off
when it has nowhere to be.
Do you have somewhere to be?

Saturn gives you a name at birth.
You are called by it. You learn to answer to it.

When Saturn returns, he asks what you've created with that name.

The ways you've used your inheritance are judged.
This is not punishment.
It is the process of becoming.

Only what is true survives.

PART THREE

(Genesis 2:1-3)

THE RETURN

Dead, Again

I was born holding a shovel
I didn't know I could put down.

Some may say I dug my own grave.

And isn't that the truth.

In the Middle of the Tunnel

RESTART.

Archive every photo you posted to get a like.
Post a new photo that you like.
Don't ask anyone if they like it, too.

REDO.

Walk back to the first doorway that you crossed
when you didn't choose yourself.
Knock and ask to try again.
The universe will always answer "yes".
She will open the door and welcome you into an empty room.
She'll hand you a pen.
She'll point towards a table that wasn't there before.
On the table, there is a blank piece of paper.

> Pick it up.
> Hold it.

Now   – try again.
Try again to choose you; not the version that'll gain the most applause
this time.
Choose the real you.
If you're still unsure of who that is, look down at the paper you're
holding.
A word will appear.

REINVENT.

When you see it, you will fall forward into a black hole forming in the
centre of the page.
It's dark for an amount of time you can't explain, until suddenly it's not.
You see yourself.

You burn all the clothes in your closet.
You stand naked in front of a mirror.
You're 28 & you notice for the first time—your ears aren't the same size.
When you notice this, you'll notice a feeling in your chest, like you're
seeing a friend you forgot you had.
It's okay to smile here.
Smile at the asymmetry.
Smile at the feeling of thinking of yourself as a phenomenal being.
Smile at the lack of guilt you feel over thinking of yourself as a
phenomenal being.
This is phenomenal. You. Just being.

And just as you grow comfortable with this image in the mirror,
you will fall forward into a black hole forming in the centre of the glass.
It's dark for an amount of time you can't explain, until suddenly it's not.

You see a caterpillar crawl into a cocoon, then turn into a Monarch.
It glides over the ocean, and up towards the sun.
It doesn't stop, until it melts into a sparrow.

The sparrow hovers in the clouds for a moment, its wings fully
expanded.
It catches your eye and winks just before it tucks itself in and dives
head first into
high waters.
Compelled, you follow it into the sea, and watch it struggle to swim
down deeper.
It holds its breath just long enough to touch its claws to the coral reef
and then it drowns.

You can't weep here, even though you want to; instead you open your
mouth and scream.
The water carries the bubbles of your grief to the surface.
The universe pulls the plug and the ocean begins to drain like a bathtub.
You and the sparrow's body are sucked into a whirlpool and swallowed
by a black hole.
It's dark for an amount of time you can't explain, until suddenly
                                                      it's not.

You're standing in a forest
and a deer with the wings of a sparrow stands, softly at your side.
Slivers of sunlight slip through the trees and touch your face.
Shyly, you look down at your muddy feet.
When you look up again, the deer darts forward—
its glorious legs spread long—you feel an urge to follow,
as you race to catch up, the trees around you bend over and lock arms.
Their leaves and trunks turn to concrete and burrow you in,
the forest floor turns to pavement and everything grows dark,
you feel a panic rise in you until your eye catches a glimmer of light at
the end of the tunnel.

You've never run as fast as you're running right now.
And when you've nearly reached that light, you realize it's attached to
the front of a pickup truck that meets the deer sprinting 10 feet ahead
of you.

I m p a c t   o c c u r s   i n   s l o w   m o t i o n .
You watch the front bumper break its body,
You watch the rubber tires feast on its flesh –
You're so hollow from watching,
that the truck roars through you like a mist.
You feel nothing.
You feel everything.
You feel the pavement beneath your feet crack,
You feel yourself in the palm of the universe's hand
as it crushes concrete to ash.

The earth absorbs your atoms into her soil
where she holds you in her arms until you remember that you are whole
and then she plants you as a cypress seedling where you will grow for
100 years
making oxygen and poetry.

Until one day, a man arrives.
He's holding a saw;
He intends to force you into a new form.
He has deemed you more valuable as a pulp,
a pulp that he will turn into slices of paper, which he will package

inside of more paper,
to sell in exchange for even more paper.
And to him, you will never be enough.

He treats you carelessly and doesn't consider that you are
the material makeup of his perceived power.

He carves away at your trunk until you snap,
and when you fall, every living being in the forest hears the sound.
They cry out for you.
As he drags your body towards merciless-man-made-machinery—
steel claws that will gnaw you into nothing.
You're staring up at the sky and
it begins to rain.
It rains and it rains and it rains
until the sounds of any man-made-machines disappear beneath the sky's
weeping.

Then   It's quiet. The most quiet it's been
since the first beginning that you can remember.
Some amount of time passes that you can't explain,
and then you find yourself as a single piece of paper,
in the hands of some kid,
who is learning to write the truth down for the first time.

She draws with a pen on the surface of your skin
and if you can manage to get a look at it,
you'll see a little caterpillar tattooed onto the center of you.

REBIRTH.

She snaps a photo of you, pauses to type a caption, and posts.

The caption says this:

> *Archive every photo you posted to get a like.*
> *Post a new photo that you like.*
> *Don't ask anyone if they like it too.*

Shame Loiters on the Other Side

If you go back to the beginning,
back to the basics,
back to every bend in the road
that I took to get here;

if you trace my steps
through every hidden door I found
in the tunnel to 29,
you'd find things I wouldn't want you to.

You'd find things I've been ashamed of,
like the lyrics
to Shane and Shane
stained
around my mouth:

> *We love you Jesus*
> *For so many reasons*
> *For death*
> *And Life*
> *And freedom—*

things I'm ashamed of,
not because I'm ashamed
of loving Jesus
for certain reasons, but,

because I'm ashamed
      of the associations attached to the labels,
      of the exclusions in organized religion,
      of the debt I owe myself, for the self betrayal,
      of believing a series of truths that never belonged to me.

The First Supper

I didn't talk at the table much this Christmas,
Grandma's glances are asking me why.

Because I don't have to.
I don't want to.
I don't owe you.

I'm home, aren't I?
I'm home. Leave me be.

The Last Supper

I didn't talk much on the car ride home to Arkansas,
my sister's questions got me thinking.

Because karma has my lips
pinched between her fingers.
And the ego never goes away, so
                how do we integrate?

I'm home and I don't want to talk about it right now,
but every time that supper bell rings,

I pull up a chair.
I use my tongue
to lick the plate
you're feeding me from
as an expression of gratitude
for six years of saving my seat,
and
because I'm hungry.
Because I want to chew.
Swallow.
Digest.
All that I missed.

What do you want me to say?
It's you that I missed.
But I don't wanna talk about it yet.

I've got to find my body first.
I've got to find the child haunting this house
with my name.

Hayley, where are you?

It's time to come out and play.   112

Prodigal Child

There's a hole
in a closet
in the bedroom
of a trailer
on a hillside
in Mississippi.

It is where I go to find her.

Because inside the hole,
inside the closet,
inside the bedroom,
inside the trailer,
on that hillside
in Mississippi

lives a memory of the name I left behind
to chase the truths I was still afraid to speak.

Every transformation costs you something,
so I gambled with what my father gave me
in search of something of my own.

And I learned,
no matter how far you stretch from the root,
stretch towards the sky,
try to stretch out the aches
from the wounds you've been avoiding for years,
the wind will always blow
and the chimes will follow,
and there will come a moment,

— when you're way up north
or way out west
or far out east —

and you're laying in bed,
and it's a summer night,
and you can almost hear your sister's voice

whispering the name your father chose,
through the hole in your closet
that she dug from her room,
asking you if you wanna go start a fire in the yard,
or run around in the trees,
or climb the roof and look for Saturn,
because on a clear night,
you can see anything from out here.

      There will come a moment,
      you're laying there
      and you'll miss it.

You'll miss hearing the name you resented
because you didn't understand how it fit,
or how you fit.

You'll miss your sister's friendship
      only a bedroom away,
you'll miss your father's assurance
      asleep in the den,
you'll miss your mother,
and your grandparents,
and your aunt
and your cousins.
You'll miss sweet tea
and corn bread
and water from the earth
and the South

and yourself.

And that feeling will carry you forward
and you'll go to that hillside,
to that trailer,
to that bedroom,
to that closet.
You'll look through that hole
and you'll find her;

      and it'll surprise you,
      the way you see each other,
      the way you want to tell each other everything.

EX CHURCH POSTER CHILD

When it comes to lore,
everyone has their side of the story.
In this one,
the Christian's will tell you I quit.
That I abandoned the flock
in pursuit of my heathen impulses,
blasphemy,
idolatry.

They'd use language like lost sheep;
or wayward son;
like *bless her heart, the world got to her*,
or the Devil himself—
or some jezebel demon—
maybe to some, I'm the demon.
I'm the wolf in sheep's clothing.
I'm the darkness you had to face.

I'm sure the Christian's prayed for me, a while.
and prayed for each other,
as they grieved the loss of their idea of me—
and in a Canadian apartment across town,
I was doing the same.

Lore is an energy,
this is how it moves.
And so we move along,
collecting fragments of stories,
piecing the puzzle together,
sifting for meaning.

When it comes to lore,
everyone has their side of the story.
Here's mine;
I didn't quit.
I tried to stay.
I washed their feet in tears,
and asked them to hear me.

But I was told to submit
a letter of resignation.

"It's best
for everyone"—

told to be careful because,
"you know how these things can get around".

told that it was not my place
to expose the youth group to what it costs
to be made in the image of a queer Jesus—
not my place to burden them.

And at the leadership meeting
where I was told I lacked integrity,
I realized who I'd given my power to –

to a man on his homemade throne,
drawing cartoon images on a paper
while his flock tore apart my character –
And I let them.

Because WWJD.

WWJD

I'd grown to believe this is what Jesus would do:

> Take it on the chin,
> turn the other cheek,
> take my heart right out of my chest
> and toss it onto the altar
> for everyone to take a bite.

They ate me alive.
And I let them.

Here's my side of the story.
I didn't lose my job because I'm gay.
I lost my job because I didn't fit the mold anymore.
Because I wouldn't play by their rules.
Because I saw the holes in their metaphors
and I called it out—
love and control are not the same.
They are enemies.

I didn't quit.
I fought for acceptance,
and forgot to fight for my own existence.
The price for that was embarrassment,
exclusion,
exile.

Just know, when it comes to lore,
everyone has a side,
an angle,
a reason below the surface

that is often hard to see.

Mine used to be survival.
Now it's me, taking my power back —
packing my bags
not because I'm running away this time
but because it's time for me to go home
to get my gun back
and to fire away with the truth.

Because WWSD.
> *What would Saturn do?*

Saturn's Interrogation

Give me a moment,
my guilt is grieving,
watching me throw every "sorry" I've ever said
into the air like confetti,
while Saturn duct tapes my shame to a chair
so I can speak with it.

There are things I insist on saying, like:

Yes, I've been out of touch
because I'm out of touch
with the scales on which we wager our expectations.
Because I'm busy
thinking about how there's a difference
between "right" and "fair".

Fair means – you need some sun in your life.
Fair means – you oughta do *this* because I did *that*.

Right means – ownership.
        as in – own your shit.
        As in, it's time to own up
        to all the ways you've spent your energy
        up to now.

Right is the justice card
turned upright on the table
for the tenth time
this week.

This week,
I realized
I'm out of touch
with every obligation I've accumulated
over three decades.
I've broken every covenant
my ego coveted
and carried for clout.

I'm over the details,
always dawning on me
two seconds, too late.
I've almost always arrived late
and hated myself for it.

But I'm here,
and I can't hate myself for it.

I've been out of touch,
figuring out how
to get over the effects
of an inner mistrust
that I once drank
from every communion cup
placed in my hands.

Give me a minute;
I'm grieving.
Releasing
all of this shit
—it doesn't belong to me.

The Final Act; No Curtain Call

Nevermind is the word I want written
in the place I go to die.

No one said it to me, but they should have:
       You're allowed to change your mind.

I'm nearly 30 now, and I am learning
how to change my mind.

I am learning to lie down,
without planning my own resurrection.

I've been back to the garden
blooming inside my stomach,
a thousand times since I left the South,
asking God for something else.

At every stage I've constructed,
when the curtain draws,
I walk laps with the kind of analysis
that stains my sheets in blood.

I sweat through my own wanting,
and every fear,
inherited or hand-carved.
Particular. Displayed
on a shelf inside my chest.

I could list them for you,
one by one,
in all their little nuances.
I could recite

their ingredients,
woven in with every verse
I memorized to survive.

I have always been afraid to die.

And I could build a castle
from the objects of my affection
collected like relics
to prove I'm still here
—and that there are reasons
to go through with it. To get on with it.

I've been carrying my cross
around in circles for years,
around walls I placed the bricks in myself,
begging God to push it over,
to show me there's a point,
or to point me in the right direction.

But I'm tired of being afraid to die,

So I'm learning to lie down,
without planning my resurrection
—without setting an alarm
on my deathbed.

I'm learning to let the truth
hit me like a whip
over and over again,
until I'm empty.

I'm learning to lie down
and let it be finished.

At the End of the Tunnel

The light will burn your eyes.
Don't look away.

Discomfort is the unfamiliar.
It's the weight of all elements combined
into one natural disaster.
Be that disaster for a minute.

Don't hide in a ditch
when you hear the sirens.
Walk into the tunnel,
let the wind thrash you into the earth,
until you learn to ride every storm
with your hands wide open.

Do not reach to grab.
There is nothing there for you to hold.

You are already holding it.
You have always been holding it.

You've died inside an ocean before,
and look at you,
     breathing.

Do it again. Sink in,
stop holding your breath.
Lay on the floor
until you can feel the gills
forming on your neck.

Then rise up, walk out of the water,
start the biggest fire you've ever seen
and stand barefoot in the centre of it.
Your skin will crawl with pain
that's been dormant for years.
Let the flames lick your wounds,

and when you finally hear
that sound in your stomach
that yells out your own name,
walk out of the fire and deep into the woods,
where there is a clearing.
Dig a hole in the ground.
Drop your shovel.

Forgive them.
Forgive yourself.

Sunrise with Saturn

(Post-return)

I'm on the beach when I finally see him.

My father – I see him,
waist deep in the ocean, standing
like Stonewall in the Civil War,
refusing to move until the storm passes,
holding his ground, stubborn for change
in the systems and structures he was given
that no longer fit.

I'm on the beach when I finally see him.

My father – inside of my own eyes
when I'm waist deep in the ocean, standing
like Stonewall in '69,
refusing to move until the storm passes,
holding my ground, stubborn for change
in the systems and structures I was given
that no longer fit.

Southern Inheritance

I was born a writer like Hemingway.

Like Hemingway, my father gave me a 20-gauge shotgun,
along with all necessary garments to blend in.

> A core concept in hunting lessons.
> A core concept in teaching a child to survive out in the woods.

I was born a writer like Fitzgerald.

Like Fitzgerald, my father builds things with his hands,
with his hands, he held our family above everything apart from God.

> A core concept in building from the dirt, up.
> A core concept in teaching a child to make meaning with chaos.

I was born a writer like Faulkner.

Like Faulkner, my father raised me in Southern soil, took me to
every battlefield to show me where someone died
for something bigger than themselves,

> A core concept in history lessons.
> A core concept in teaching a child that every breath from their
> own lungs
>
>   is a breath from the whole.

Today My Father Called

to ask me how I wanted to celebrate my 30th birthday.
So I told him.

I said Daddy –
I want to meet you at the half way point
on this mountain we've been going round for years –
missing each other at every check point,
two steps ahead
or two seconds too late.

I'm at the peak now and
I wanna come down to rest.
I wanna come down,
and meet you half way.

I wanna go back to that place
that you took us as kids,
in middle of Arkansas,
hidden in the Ozarks,
where the springs run warm
and the trees whisper stories.

I wanna go back to where you carried us,
let us dip our toes into hot water
to test our toughness.
We'd get up to our ankles
and laugh in harmony with the hurt.
Together in the mountains.
You taught us to make friends with discomfort.

I'm coming down the mountain.
I'm coming to the half way point
to meet you in that place,
where you gave your love to us
through trading the dollar bills
you had to break your back to earn
for the kind of memories in childhood
that made us feel like we had everything—
and believe we could have anything—
where roller coasters weren't just roller coasters,
they were rocket ships to a world where we were free,
and carnival games weren't just games,
they were negotiations with fate.
You taught us to bet on what we believe in,
and you believed in us.

You pulled every buck from your wallet
to win a stuffed animal,
because we don't quit until we win.
So we win.

It's because of you, I have won.
Because you are the father,
Because you have been the son,
Because I am your spirit living on.

You called me to tell me you were coming up the mountain.
You were coming to the half way point, to see me,
that you were leaving everything on hold, to hold space for us.

You told me that you regret
how you let work take you away from us
when we were young.
You told me you feel like you missed out on so much.
You told me you are proud of us.
And you hadn't taken a Sunday off in years and they'd be okay without
you.

You said I only turn 30 once.
And you're right.
You've always been right about these kinds of things.

And I *know* you're right because now I am
where you've been before
and I can meet you back at that place,
the place you've always been coming from.

I can meet at that half way point on this mountain
to tell you I found my way home.

Saturn Loves Me

Even When He Doesn't Understand Me

Used to, living with my father,
he'd come to my bedroom door,
and lean his head in
sometime after dinner,
after a day's work was done,
while Momma was cleaning the kitchen,
and I was knee deep in my own world
—in a pile of toys on the floor—

he'd say, "I'm gonna rent this movie if you wanna come watch."

Or – "I'm gonna watch this show, if you wanna come to the
living room and hang out."

Or – "the football game is on, come help me coach them through
the tv"
[because we're Dallas fans—fuck the haters]

he'd make some offer, a Capricorn kind of barter, like
If you'll sit here with me, I'll rent this movie or 10 movies,
Money is no object, if it'll buy him some of my time.

I watched a lot of movies growing up.
Half of my DNA is made up of glorified heroes
and misunderstood villains.
The angel and the devil living on my shoulders at all times—
this used to bug me.

These days, I live with my sister,
And sometimes she comes to my bedroom door

and leans her head in,
sometime after dinner
after a day's work is done
while I pet my cat or water my plant
and get knee deep in my own loneliness—
in a pile of memories on the floor—

> She'll say, "Drag Race is on this week, if you wanna come
> watch."
> Or – "I'm about to watch American Horror Story,
> if you wanna come to the living room and hang out."
> Or – "I'm gonna invite people over to play Jackbox, come out
> here and help me host."
> [because we are our momma's daughters]

She'll make some offer, a Capricorn kind of barter, like
if you'll sit here with me, I'll get this streaming service or 10.
Money is no object, if it'll buy her some of my time.

I've seen a lot of TV lately, that I've only half paid attention to,
but I've noticed,
half of my DNA is made up of scripted realities and
truths told through fiction.
The angel and the devil live on my shoulder at all times,
but this no longer bugs me.
It's how I know love.

I know love because
> I am the sister
> *and* the daughter
> of a Capricorn;
> from a long lineage of magic, power, and   loyalty.

> And I am loved.
> Because of them, I am love.

Revival

I close my eyes and wake up at 5pm
in the fall of 2025.
My sister is jumping on my bed
telling me it's time to get up, it's *Sunday*.

>We're around the table
>eating breakfast, as the sun is going down,
>in an old garden, revived
>by the hands of our honesty.

I close my eyes and stretch out
into the soft arms of the sabbath.
My sister is 31 and she teaches me,

>that Sunday is like an open field,
>where we lay down
>and roll around
>or roll a joint and bake
>in the center of a sunset.

>She was born a step ahead,
>I was born a quick learner.

I close my eyes and wake up and
it's quiet—like
I can finally breathe again and
I watch the grass grow,
while I drink a coffee and
then go for a drive down a backroad
with my oldest friend.

This is a form of healing.
It's the sound of the crickets on my windowsill
in a double wide, in the boondocks,
down a gravel road
that looks different to me now.

It's taking ownership of my own emotions
that have always been mine to carry.
And in the middle of nowhere,
I am the one that will.

30

I spent almost all of my 20s
trying to figure out
how to make everything perfect for my 30s.

The day I'm writing this,
I'm 19 days from 30
and I'm happy to report
that everything is so marvelously
         imperfect;
so beautifully and wonderfully
         flawed.

What an image –
watching life unfold honestly
like watching God
paint a mural
on live stream.

Today I'm 19 days from 30,
and by the time I read this to you
I'll already be there,
out in the light,
out of the long, dark tunnel that is your 20s,
out in the open air.

I'm writing this down to clear the air
for all of the ones who've been stuck
         holding it in,
         holding it together,
         holding the trauma
         inside your lungs

to avoid the screams.
Holding the questions
because both silence and response
are scary.

.

.

.

Permission. to breathe.

To be afraid and not judge yourself for it,
to not hate yourself this time.

Permission to take up space,
in this room and
that other room
you've been avoiding
because it makes you feel small.

It is you –
allowing someone else
to wrap their fingers around your throat,
or to slide their hand up your shirt
and use your mouth to speak.

Your power is to speak, but
you've been holding your breath.
Stop. Breathe *with* me.
And think
about that time,

When you were 8
and someone asked you a question
beyond the reach of your intricately learned
and highly developed moral compass,
		so you answered by the truth
		found in your stomach.

You thought you were wrong but you weren't.

Or that time, when you were 12
and it happened again.
Or 17. Or 21. Or 25. or now.

You think you are wrong, but you aren't.
That nudge in your stomach.
Listen.

I spent almost all of my 20s
getting ready for today.

And after all I've collected
in a decade of life,
I've brought very little with me.
But I'm ready.

Saturn Direct

It's Day 7.

The day God puts the pencil down and says,
"Well, let's see what becomes of this".

I'm putting my pencil down.
Whatever may become of this.

It's the end and so –
It's the beginning.
When it's all just an idea
swimming inside the mind of God—
a thread in the void, and then,
                    there is light.
                    And when the light comes,
                    so does the rest.

333

ENCORE

A Postface for Fayetteville

For a very long time, I couldn't see it,
but then I dusted off my Bible and I saw it –
Revelation reincarnated;
a new sky;
a new world;
the old world—gone.
The lakes and the ponds—dissolved.
Reality, swallowed
into its own stomach;
a black hole;
a long dark tunnel
of inherited desires, ancestral trauma,
undiscussed misunderstandings, and stubborn
Southern-American ignorance,
churning in acid,
digesting,
absorbed in my own
carefully, curated *just-for-you*, world—
      the old world—
       gone. Empty now.

And then I saw it: the new Jerusalem, the Holy city, on the hill
—a new community—descending out of the heavens from God,
draped in Cardinal Red.

I saw it on the other side of the tunnel;
I followed the light,
and the crickets,
and the sound of my inner child

until I reached the center,
where I heard a strong voice,
coming from a dive bar
on Dickson St., in Fayetteville, Arkansas.

I heard the voice say, "Look!
You are home now.
        At home with God.
        At home with your father.
        At home with Saturn.
        At home with the South.
        At home with yourself,
                and the kind of ownership
                that holds the power
                to build kingdoms
                or tear them down."

It was a familiar voice,
I heard saying,
"They will know your power by your love.
By the bridges you build *and*
the bridges you burn,
        knowing why.

The old world is gone.
The old order of things has ended.
Energy is the new currency."

And then the voice said, "Look,
I am making all things new,
write this down,
because these words can be trusted.
They are true."

Thank you, Fayetteville,
for holding me.
For loving me before you even knew me.
For loving me still, now that you do.
I have found refuge in you.

With love,

B. Davis

This piece of writing was intentionally mirrored after

Revelations 21:1-5 (NIV)

THANK YOU— FOR REAL

When I began this journey, the work was something entirely different than it is now. I remember the day I decided to write this book. I remember where I was, who was there, and where I sat, as I wrote the first 3 poems in minutes. It fell on me like lightning, at first. And then it came in waves over the course of 3 years.

I've spent 3 years writing this, living in 2 different countries at various points – so there are a lot of people whose energy has touched this work.

To the people that have held space for me to unravel and come undone time and time again, to the people who've listened to every breakthrough, epiphany, breakdown, or obsessive rant, that I have had, and most of all, those of you who have looked at my work, then looked at me, and demanded me to keep trying until I finally told the real, raw truth – thank you.

◆

Here's an overview of some of the people who helped me make this happen, and how we spent some of our time together.

Shelby Davis — also known as "the cult leader", "the goddess of taverns and ales", and perhaps to people who know nothing beyond the rumors they choose to listen to—she's the Devil card turned upright on their table. But I have always known her as my big sister. My only sister. My best friend.

If she didn't exist, neither would this book.
For every line I was too afraid to write, she knew exactly how to pull it out of me.

If I call this book my child, she is the godparent. You will find her finger prints within these pages.

My sister deserves her own book. And one day, I'll write that book. But until then, I want the world to know that I wouldn't be the person I am today if it weren't for her. It is because of her that I still believe in the existence of unconditional love.

And in many ways, this book is an offering to her – a relic of the love she has invested in me all of my life, coming to the surface; so the world may see the power of choosing someone for who they are. Not for who you want them to be.

Douha Al Wahidi — She was there the day the book began. She was standing in the kitchen, making coffee, when I caught the idea like a fever and sat at the kitchen island with a pen and started to write. I wrote 3 poems that day and read them aloud to her.

From that day forward, she fanned the flame in me, every time the work was on the edge of being extinguished.

Every single time I considered throwing it out and walking away, she would let me borrow some of her courage. It is because of her that I found the endurance and grit inside myself to see this through to the end. She refused to let me give up. And there is nothing of equal value to exchange for this gift.

She has seen all 13 manuscripts of this work – read every single one of
the dozens of poems that didn't even make the cut, much less the ones
that remain. She has edited, nourished, and carried the weight of this
work with me from beginning to end.

If you know Douha, you're one of the lucky ones. If you don't—I pray
one day you find a Douha.

I've never met anyone more willing to go to the ends of the Earth to
help their loved ones survive, process, and heal the jungle of pain that
lives [uniquely] within each of us.

The Boys — I met "the boys" because my last two years in Hamilton,
I took a job bartending and they became my coworkers. It was a small
staff, so we spent a lot of time together. These two were like finding
shade in the desert. They took me under their wings, protected me,
loved me—saw me—let me exist, in all my whimsical wanderings and
wonderings. And they would walk with me, through every mental maze
I brought to them (which, eventually, was basically everyday).

Alex & Nathan. They became my **brothers**. A term I hadn't really been
willing to use since I lost my job at the church. They washed that word
clean for me.

And Alex, a poet himself, came to me with the idea to do cocktails and
poetry. So poetry night was born, and we all worked together to bring
it to life. Each time we did it, there was hardly room to stand. Seasoned
poets and new writers alike got up on the mic. It was a dream come
true, to be honest. Something that felt like it could only happen in the
movies—happening right there in our city—because of the Boys and
the bar and all of those poets who came from within and beyond our
city to be together.

My Hamilton Workshop Crew — they would come over and let me feed them pizza and beers in exchange for workshopping 3-5 poems every week. This was early on in the book's becoming, and the memories of it sit warmly with me – because these are the folks who showed up for me when I was still struggling to show up for myself. We'd sit in a circle in the living room and they'd let me pace the floor trying to get up the courage to read the poems aloud for the first time. The following list are the names of anyone who showed up to [at least] one of these sessions. Thank y'all for showing up and believing in me:

Douha Al Wahidi
Michelle Boyle
Esmae Ali
Sierra Knowles
Kieran Thiara
Laura Heaney
Paul Watson
Keira Killin
Alicia Moores
Sarah Robinson
Emma Mckinnon
Monica Mcdonald
Alex Drumm

Monday Press — this is an artist collective in Hamilton, Ontario, that was born inside of a laundromat. I don't believe in accidents, but crossing paths with Monday Press was nothing short of a miracle for me and my journey as an artist. These are the kinds of people they make movies about 50 years after the revolution, when people finally realize it was the artists that changed the world—not the government. If you are an artist looking for places to make honest art with other artists – check them out. They are the real deal.

Instagram: @monday.press

Extra (I promised my Leo moon the last word)

To the Southern Baptist Church—Jesus is not a renewable resource
you can monopolize and use to gain power and control the world.
According to scripture, He is the son of God, born a Jew to the Virgin
Mary. Remember, it was the Jewish temple leaders who crucified him.

If you are reading this as a member of an SBC church, this is not
directed at you – it is directed at the men who have chosen to establish
and maintain the status quo that you live under. If you are offended, I
understand. I once was offended by things like this too. (We are often
offended by things that are true. See Bible for examples).

To the THF leadership team — you submit your will to a bully. And
in turn, you become complicit in the harm caused to anyone who crosses
your church's path, that challenges or questions your indoctrinated
thoughts, beliefs, and theology.

You choose funding (money and security) over your "people" or "family".
You live in fear of the system you operate within, and you are raising
and teaching your children to do the same.

I never asked you to change your minds about queer people. I just
needed you to listen to my heart and you couldn't. You saw the worst in
me and since I was unwilling to submit to your mindset, you abandoned
me.

How many more will you abandon for the same reasons?

How many of you will abandon yourself, for the same reasons?